Action

Poems

Mary Colson

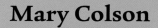

KT-574-313

Raintree is an imprint of Capstone Global Library Limited, a company incorporated in England and Wales having its registered office at 7 Pilgrim Street, London, EC4V 6LB – Registered company number: 6695582

www.raintreepublishers.co.uk
myorders@raintreepublishers.co.uk

Text © Capstone Global Library Limited 2014
First published in hardback in 2014
The moral rights of the proprietor have been asserted.

Produced for Raintree by
White-Thomson Publishing
www.wtpub.co.uk
+44 (0)843 208 7460

Edited by Claudia Martin
Cover design by Tim Mayer
Designed by Alix Wood
Concept design by Alix Wood

Production by Victoria Fitzgerald
Originated by Capstone Global Library Ltd
Printed and bound in China

ISBN 978 1 4062 7289 5
17 16 15 14 13
10 9 8 7 6 5 4 3 2 1

British Library Cataloguing in Publication Data
A full catalogue record for this book is available from the British Library.

Disclaimer
All the internet addresses (URLs) given in this book were valid at the time of going to press. However, due to the dynamic nature of the internet, some addresses may have changed, or sites may have changed or ceased to exist since publication. While the author and publisher regret any inconvenience this may cause readers, no responsibility for any such changes can be accepted by either the author or the publisher.

CONTENTS

Experiencing action poetry

What do you think poetry is? Quite simply, poetry is an idea or a story expressed in a very **economical** way, using words, sound effects, techniques, and emotion. There are often certain "ingredients" that we expect in a poem, like rhyme or the way it looks on the page, but there are not any fixed rules. As you will see from the poems in this book, poetry can take many forms and use many different ideas and techniques.

What can "action" mean?

The poems in this book are all concerned with different aspects of the **theme** of action. When you think of the word "action", what do you think of? What are its **connotations**? It is helpful to consider what this word might mean before you read any of the poems.

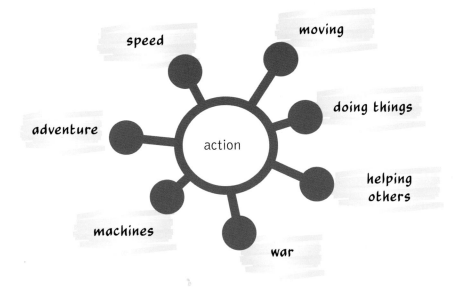

Actions can be physical movements, like dropping a cup on the floor, or something grander, like protesting in a crowd and waving banners against something you think is wrong. As you read the poems in this book, think about all the different ways that actions can be done. Sometimes, people act to protect themselves and sometimes they act to protect others. Actions can be brave, violent, romantic, and mechanical. Sometimes, as you will see in the poem "Not My Business" (on page 45), even doing nothing is a form of action.

Background and influences

Every poem is written in a particular time and place or situation. This is called the **context**. For example, imagine a poet is writing during a time of war. This will probably influence his or her writing and produce certain ideas, attitudes, and responses. The context may even inspire a poet to write in the first place. Imagine that same poet lost somebody special in the war: how do you think that loss might affect their poetry?

A survival guide to poetry

There is no need to panic when you are faced with a poem. One of the first ways of getting into a poem is to make a PACT with it. A pact is an agreement and, if you make a PACT with a poem, you'll always be able to draw something out of it. Try to answer the following questions:

P – purpose: what is the poem's purpose?
A – audience: who is the poem's audience?
C – context: what is the poem's context?
T – theme: what is the poem's theme?

Whatever the subject and whoever the writer, every poem has a purpose, or a "message" for the reader or audience. The poet will have chosen their words and techniques very carefully and deliberately in order to get that message across. By looking closely at a poem, these techniques can be picked out.

What does the word "action" mean to you – speed, getting involved, excitement?

How to approach a poem

When you look at a poem, do you often feel as if you are being tricked or that you will think the wrong thing about it? Lots of people feel this way. First of all, take your time reading the poem. Is there a line you like or a particular word that stands out? Perhaps an image reminds you of something. It might be the title that strikes you, or you might think about when the poem was written or when it is set.

A good way to start exploring a poem is to pick out some images that you think are particularly striking. Try drawing these images on a piece of paper. Do they form a contrast with each other? What are the differences between your images? The poet chose those images on purpose to make an impression on the reader: what impression did they make on you?

Reading for meaning

When you first approach a poem, it is important to read it to get the general feel, and then you can re-read and try to pick out more details. It is always possible to understand something about a poem. It might be the main idea, or theme, running through it, or where it is set.

As you read the poems in this book, ask yourself the following questions. If you can answer some of them, you are on your way to understanding the poem's content and the poet's message.

- Who is narrating the poem?
- Whose point of view is it from?
- What emotions are present?
- What is the theme?
- What do you think the poet is trying to achieve?
- What does the poet want the reader to feel or think?

"You" and the audience

Believe it or not, you might not be the intended audience of a poem. Poets sometimes direct their words at a general reader, but often they are aiming at a specific audience. A poem's audience may depend on the message the poet wants to get across. It could be a poem warning a child about danger, or a poem aimed at politicians or protesters about making the right choices.

It is helpful to work out who you think the poet is addressing as this will help you to work out the message or theme of the poem. For example, if the poem has an anti-war message, perhaps the audience is meant to be the military leaders who make the decisions that affect soldiers' lives. Think about all the possible people the poet is aiming his or her words at. Doing this will help you to understand more about the tone and mood of the poem, too.

Why write poems?

Many poets write because they have an important message to convey, while other poets write about historical events or important people. Sometimes poets are inspired by heroic actions. At other times, they may feel it is their duty to record events or how people are feeling. As you read the poems in this book, think about what may have **motivated** the poet to write. Are they writing to raise awareness? To warn? To mourn? To help change their audience's mind?

On 6 September 2002, the American poet Billy Collins read his poem "The Names" to an audience of the United States **Congress**. The poem honoured the victims of the 11 September 2001 attacks. But was his poem's intended audience larger than just the Congress?

TITLE CLUES

It is easy to overlook poem titles, but very often, the more you explore the title, the more you understand the poem. Titles can get your ideas churning, thoughts spinning, and predictions whirring before you have even read a line. Sometimes titles tell us about the specific action that is happening ("Paul Revere's Ride" on page 9), while others suggest something more **abstract** ("Acts of God" on page 33). Look back at this book's contents list on page 3 and consider what you think the poems might be about. Can you predict the mood of the poems?

"Paul Revere's Ride"

In April 1775, the United States and Britain were heading for war. Until then, the 13 original American states were British **colonies** ruled from London. The states wanted independence, and so began a bloody war that was to last for eight years – until independence was granted in 1783. Henry Wadsworth Longfellow was inspired to write this poem by the events of the night of 18–19 April 1775, in the hours leading up to the first shots of the **War of Independence**.

The story of the poem

The American colonists had heard that the British were planning an attack. Paul Revere, who was a citizen of Boston, Massachusetts, had helped organize an alarm system to alert the colonists to the movements of the British military. In the poem, Revere tells a friend to go to the Old North Church tower in Boston and light signal lanterns. These lanterns will let Revere know whether the British are attacking by land or sea. Revere waits across the river in Charlestown. When he sees two lanterns, Revere knows the British are coming by sea. He quickly rides through the towns listed in the poem to warn people.

WORDS YOU MAY NOT KNOW

belfry: bell tower of a church
man-of-war: warship
sentinel: guard or lookout
impetuous: acting on the spur of the moment, on impulse
spectral: ghostly
fleet: fast, rapid
British Regulars: professional soldiers
redcoats: British soldiers serving overseas in former times

Paul Revere rowed across the Charles River, from Boston to Charlestown, between 10 and 11 p.m. on 18 April 1775.

"Paul Revere's Ride"

by Henry Wadsworth Longfellow

Listen my children and you shall hear
Of the midnight ride of Paul Revere,
On the eighteenth of April, in Seventy-five:
Hardly a man is now alive
Who remembers that famous day and year.

He said to his friend, "If the British march
By land or sea from the town to-night,
Hang a lantern aloft in the belfry arch
Of the North Church tower as a signal
    light,–
One if by land, and two if by sea;
And I on the opposite shore will be,
Ready to ride and spread the alarm
Through every Middlesex village and farm,
For the country folk to be up and to arm."

Then he said "Good-night!" and with
    muffled oar
Silently rowed to the Charlestown shore,
Just as the moon rose over the bay,
Where swinging wide at her moorings lay
The Somerset, British man-of-war:
A phantom ship, with each mast and spar
Across the moon like a prison bar,
And a huge black hulk, that was magnified
By its own reflection in the tide.

Meanwhile, his friend, through alley and
    street
Wanders and watches, with eager ears,
Till in the silence around him he hears
The muster of men at the barrack door,
The sound of arms, and the tramp of feet,
And the measured tread of the grenadiers,
Marching down to their boats on the shore.

Then he climbed the tower of the Old
    North Church,
By the wooden stairs, with stealthy tread,

To the belfry chamber overhead,
And startled the pigeons from their perch
On the sombre rafters, that round him
    made
Masses and moving shapes of shade, –
By the trembling ladder, steep and tall,
To the highest window in the wall,
Where he paused to listen and look down
A moment on the roofs of the town
And the moonlight flowing over all.

Beneath, in the churchyard, lay the dead,
In their night encampment on the hill,
Wrapped in silence so deep and still
That he could hear, like a sentinel's tread,
The watchful night-wind, as it went
Creeping along from tent to tent,
And seeming to whisper, "All is well!"
A moment only he feels the spell
Of the place and the hour, and the secret
    dread
Of the lonely belfry and the dead;
For suddenly all his thoughts are bent
On a shadowy something far away,
Where the river widens to meet the bay, –
A line of black that bends and floats
On the rising tide like a bridge of boats.

Meanwhile, impatient to mount and ride,
Booted and spurred, with a heavy stride
On the opposite shore walked Paul Revere.
Now he patted his horse's side,
Now he gazed at the landscape far and
    near,
Then, impetuous, stamped the earth,
And turned and tightened his saddle girth;
But mostly he watched with eager search
The belfry tower of the Old North Church,
As it rose above the graves on the hill,
Lonely, and spectral, and sombre, and still.

Continued over the page

And lo! as he looks, on the belfry's height
A glimmer, and then a gleam of light!
He springs to the saddle, the bridle he
    turns,
But lingers and gazes, till full on his sight
A second lamp in the belfry burns.

A hurry of hoofs in a village street,
A shape in the moonlight, a bulk in the
    dark,
And beneath, from the pebbles, in
    passing, a spark
Struck out by a steed flying fearless and
    fleet:
That was all! And yet, through the gloom
    and the light,
The fate of a nation was riding that night;
And the spark struck out by that steed, in
    his flight,
Kindled the land into flame with its heat.
He has left the village and mounted the
    steep,
And beneath him, tranquil and broad and
    deep,
Is the Mystic, meeting the ocean tides;
And under the alders that skirt its edge,
Now soft on the sand, now loud on the
    ledge,
Is heard the tramp of his steed as he rides.

It was twelve by the village clock
When he crossed the bridge into Medford
    town.
He heard the crowing of the cock,
And the barking of the farmer's dog,
And felt the damp of the river fog,
That rises after the sun goes down.

It was one by the village clock,
When he galloped into Lexington.
He saw the gilded weathercock
Swim in the moonlight as he passed,
And the meeting-house windows, black
    and bare,
Gaze at him with a spectral glare,
As if they already stood aghast
At the bloody work they would look upon.

It was two by the village clock,
When he came to the bridge in Concord
    town.
He heard the bleating of the flock,
And the twitter of birds among the trees,
And felt the breath of the morning breeze
Blowing over the meadow brown.
And one was safe and asleep in his bed
Who at the bridge would be first to fall,
Who that day would be lying dead,
Pierced by a British musket ball.

You know the rest. In the books you have
    read
How the British Regulars fired and fled, –
How the farmers gave them ball for ball,
From behind each fence and farmyard
    wall,
Chasing the redcoats down the lane,
Then crossing the fields to emerge again
Under the trees at the turn of the road,
And only pausing to fire and load.

So through the night rode Paul Revere;
And so through the night went his cry of
    alarm
To every Middlesex village and farm, –
A cry of defiance, and not of fear,
A voice in the darkness, a knock at the
    door,
And a word that shall echo for evermore!
For, borne on the night-wind of the Past,
Through all our history, to the last,
In the hour of darkness and peril and need,
The people will waken and listen to hear
The hurrying hoof-beats of that steed,
And the midnight message of Paul Revere.

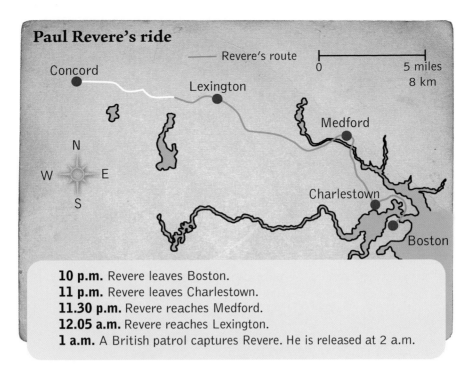

Paul Revere's ride

Revere's route

0   5 miles
           8 km

Concord

Lexington

Medford

N
W — E
S

Charlestown

Boston

10 p.m. Revere leaves Boston.
11 p.m. Revere leaves Charlestown.
11.30 p.m. Revere reaches Medford.
12.05 a.m. Revere reaches Lexington.
1 a.m. A British patrol captures Revere. He is released at 2 a.m.

The poem's PACT

The poem begins with the reader being spoken to: "listen my children". The narrator is aware of his role in telling an exciting tale to an audience. The narrator tells us that the story is set in 1775 and that the "midnight ride" is "famous". Within the opening lines of the poem, then, the reader knows the poem's PACT. The purpose is to tell the dramatic story of Paul Revere; the audience is the reader; the context is the historical battle between the United States and Britain; but what do you think the theme is?

The theme is the main idea that runs throughout a poem. "Paul Revere's Ride" is about a dramatic, heroic ride, but the main idea is of being **patriotic** (devoted to one's country). Paul Revere takes action to protect and defend his country. Look back and try to list each of the actions taken that night by Revere and his friend.

While you are thinking about the poem's theme and purpose, consider the time gap between the actions of Paul Revere in 1775 and when Longfellow wrote the poem in 1860. By 1860, America was on the verge of **civil war**. Longfellow predicts an "hour of darkness" if the civil war breaks up the Union of American states. The poet perhaps wants people "to hear" Paul Revere's "midnight message" again, and hopes to bring Americans back together and avoid war.

Action and movement

This poem has two centres of contrasting action: there is the waiting and watching to see what the British will do; and there is the galloping ride of Revere. As Paul Revere waits with his horse, at the start of **stanza** 7, he is described as being "impatient to mount and ride". Look at the words used to describe his movements as he nervously waits for the signal. We are told that he "walked", "patted", and "stamped the earth" before he "springs to the saddle" and rides off.

Many of the words used by Longfellow help to give the poem its tremendous sense of movement and haste. Look at the spider diagram below to see some examples of Longfellow's action words. Think about the drama and type of movement of each word. Some words reflect faster actions than others:

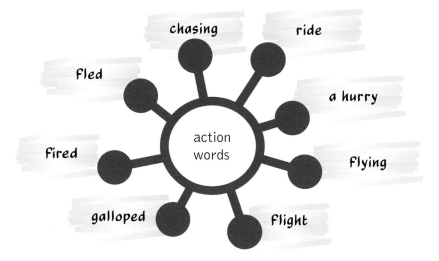

FINDING INSPIRATION

Henry Wadsworth Longfellow was inspired to write "Paul Revere's Ride" after visiting the Old North Church in Boston. He climbed the church tower and looked out over the bay. Allowing his imagination to run wild, he thought about Paul Revere and the night of his dramatic ride. Longfellow pictured the British fleet lurking below, ready to attack, and began composing the poem in his mind. He sat down and started writing it the very next day.

Tempo and beat

Poets have all sorts of ways of making their poems come alive. All words have a beat, or rhythm, and a **tempo**, or speed. Poets play with these beats and speeds to create rhythms. This might be a regular rhythm or an irregular rhythm, depending on the effect the poet is aiming for. Try reading different stanzas of "Paul Revere's Ride" out loud. Can you hear where you put emphasis on a word or a **syllable**? Try clapping your hands in time with these stressed syllables. What actions does the rhythm sound like? A train, a river, a horse? What is it likely to sound like, given the poem's title? What speed is the rhythm going? Why might a fast speed be important in this poem?

HENRY WADSWORTH LONGFELLOW

1807–1882

Born: Portland, Maine, USA

Longfellow lived in Europe as a young man, becoming fluent in a number of languages. After returning to the USA, he settled in Cambridge, Massachusetts, where he taught at Harvard University.

Did you know? In 1861, Longfellow's wife died after her dress accidentally caught fire. After this tragedy, Longfellow could not write poetry for a long time. He spent most of the rest of his life working on translations of other poets' work.

Longfellow's most famous poem is The Song of Hiawatha, which is about a legendary American Indian warrior.

Paul Revere (1734–1818) was a wealthy and respected silversmith in Boston, Massachusetts. In this 1770 painting, the artist John Singleton Copley shows him holding some of his own silverwork.

Sound effects

Traditionally, poems are meant to be spoken aloud, so they often use a range of sound effects to create an atmosphere or feeling that suits the poem's setting or actions. This might be rushing water, or a horse's hooves as the animal gallops. Say "hurry of hoofs" out loud. What effect does the sound have? Now try saying "flying fearless and fleet". What do you notice about these phrases? The poet is using **alliteration** (repetition of the same letter or sound at the beginnings of words) as a way of running the words into each other as if they are all one movement or action. Try to identify some more examples of alliteration in the poem.

Think about this
Did Longfellow tell the whole truth?

Thanks to Longfellow's poem, generations of people have grown up believing that Paul Revere was the only hero that night in 1775, but he did not act alone. Longfellow used some historical facts and also used **poetic licence**. The poem made Paul Revere a national hero, but there were several other, equally heroic, riders that night. For example, William Dawes rode with Revere, but because Longfellow did not include him in the poem, he has almost been forgotten. Paul Revere did not actually reach Concord that night, as he was captured by the British (and soon released) on the road between Lexington and Concord. Is there a danger that we take poetry as fact? Do you think that poets have to tell the whole truth about historical events?

The writer's viewpoint

When the narrator says, "You know the rest. In the books you have read..." there is an assumption that the reader is already familiar with the history of the War of Independence and the actions of Paul Revere. Most American schoolchildren know the story well, but most British children do not. The narrator is an American and a **patriot**, and he is assuming that his readers are as well.

The reader sees the action of the poem from a single point of view. Whether we are observing the heroic dash through the countryside or being told that the "British fired and fled", we are only given the story from the American perspective. The reader is clearly meant to think the British were cowardly. Imagine how the poem would be if it were written from the point of view of one of the British soldiers. Working out a poem's point of view is useful in exploring its action, message, and purpose.

In this painting by the American artist John Trumbull (1756–1843), American forces can be seen in deadly hand-to-hand combat with British redcoats.

"Anthem for Doomed Youth"

"Anthem for Doomed Youth" is the English poet Wilfred Owen's powerful and **emotive** response to the horrific actions of World War I (1914–1918). Read the poem aloud. As you do so, think about the warlike actions described. What objects of war are depicted? How do they move or sound?

Actions and consequences

What different actions can you find in the poem? Make a list on a piece of paper. Is there a difference between the kinds of actions in stanza one and those in stanza two? Think about why that might be. Does the poet want to create a contrast between the two sets of actions? Stanza one is about the bloody actions of war, while stanza two is about the consequences of those actions.

The first stanza of the poem is also full of contrasting actions. Owen refers to "choirs", which makes the reader think of beautiful, harmonious music; but we also have the ugly squeals of "wailing shells". We have prayers for the soldiers ("their hasty orisons"); but we also have the rattling of rifles. In each case, these two contrasting actions are put next to each other to make the reader feel the chaos, ugliness, and destruction of war. Can you see any other contrasting actions in the poem?

WORDS YOU MAY NOT KNOW

passing-bells: bells rung to announce a death or a funeral
orisons: prayers
demented: insane, wild
shells: explosions or bombs
pallor: paleness
pall: cloth used to cover a coffin
drawing-down of blinds: traditional mark of respect when someone has died

"Anthem for Doomed Youth"

by Wilfred Owen

What passing-bells for these who die as cattle?
Only the monstrous anger of the guns.
Only the stuttering rifles' rapid rattle
Can patter out their hasty orisons.
No mockeries for them from prayers or bells,
Nor any voice of mourning save the choirs,—
The shrill, demented choirs of wailing shells;
And bugles calling for them from sad shires.

What candles may be held to speed them all?
Not in the hands of boys, but in their eyes
Shall shine the holy glimmers of goodbyes.
The pallor of girls' brows shall be their pall;
Their flowers the tenderness of silent minds,
And each slow dusk a drawing-down of blinds.

WILFRED OWEN

1893–1918

Born: Oswestry, Shropshire, UK

Wilfred Owen signed up to join the British Army in 1915. Britain, France, and several other countries (and, from 1917, the USA) were battling against Germany in what we now call World War I. Owen was killed in northern France a week before the war ended.

Did you know? Some of Owen's poems, including "Anthem for Doomed Youth", were set to music by the composer Benjamin Britten in his *War Requiem* (1962). The **requiem** tells of the pity and waste of war.

In 1917, Owen suffered shell shock and was sent to hospital in Scotland to get better. It was there that he wrote much of his poetry.

Owen's purpose, audience, and context

It is clear from the poem's title that the purpose of "Anthem for Doomed Youth" is to inform the reader of the waste of war. The intended audience is anyone who is not there on the battlefield, witnessing the horror for themselves. The context of the poem is World War I. Wilfred Owen wrote many poems about the suffering of soldiers during the war. He often contrasts the patriotic hopes and dreams of the brave young men with the grim reality of life on the battlefield. As Owen himself died in action, it is as if "Anthem for Doomed Youth" is *his* story too. The poem has become Owen's own **epitaph**.

What is the poem's theme?

Look again at the poem. Can you spot any groups of words all connected with the same theme? One group of words is linked with weapons: "guns", "rifles' rapid rattle", and "wailing shells". A group of words that work together on a theme is called a **semantic field**. Owen also uses another group of words. Consider these words and what theme they are linked to: "passing-bells", "orisons", "prayers", "mourning", "bells", "choirs", "bugles", "candles", "holy", "flowers", "drawing-down of blinds".

They are all linked to funerals. The poem opens with a reference to funeral bells ("passing-bells"), a slow, respectful ring, and ends with blinds being drawn, a **metaphor** (when two things are compared with each other, or one is used to **symbolize** the other) for someone's death. An anthem is usually a celebratory song like a national anthem, but Owen's anthem acts as a **eulogy**, a funeral address for those who will have none. It was not possible to hold a normal funeral for those who died in battle: millions of soldiers had to be buried in huge military cemeteries (pictured) close to where they fell. The sounds of guns and shells must replace prayers and choirs.

Think about this

Is it a sonnet?

The poem has the structure of a **sonnet**, a traditional love poem. A sonnet has 14 lines and 10 syllables per line. Does Owen strictly follow this form? Look at the words "flowers" and "stuttering": how many syllables do they have? Traditionally, sonnets end with a **couplet** (a pair of lines that usually rhyme and are the same length) that "sums up" or revises what has been described. Look at the final couplet in "Anthem for Doomed Youth". How does it contrast with or sum up the rest of the poem? Why do you think Owen does not follow the traditional sonnet form? What might he be saying about war and the way it destroys things?

Writing about war

Poets have been writing about war and conflict for thousands of years. War poems can be written from many different perspectives, from the soldier in the trench, to the loved-one left at home, to the general planning the attacks a long way from the action.

It is useful to compare the action in "Anthem for Doomed Youth" with the action in another war poem, "Paul Revere's Ride" (on page 9). While Longfellow is praising the heroic actions of Revere, Owen is mourning the lack of dignity for the war's dead – "these who die as cattle". Much of the fighting in World War I was done from muddy trenches dug into the ground, which contrasts strongly with Revere's "flying" horse. The two stanzas of Owen's poem begin with questions. The rest of each stanza is an answer to those questions, with Owen's bitter attitude to war clear in his tone. "Anthem for Doomed Youth" is an anti-war poem.

In real life, Wilfred Owen acted in two ways. On the one hand, he continued to fight bravely. On the other, he acted by using poetry to inform people back home what war was really like. Today, wars are fought very differently. There are more machines and fewer soldiers. This also changes the way poets write about war.

World War I British gunners are targetting a German plane, using a Vickers machine gun and a telescope. Soldiers faced attacks from enemy soldiers, artillery, and aeroplanes.

THE SOUND OF WHISPERS

Read "Anthem for Doomed Youth" aloud one more time. Think about the sounds the words make. Are the sounds of the second stanza different from those of the first? What's different about them? The soft "s" sounds that you can hear in the second stanza are rather like whispers. When someone dies, people tend to lower their voices as a mark of respect. Wilfred Owen is doing just that here. The soft sounds of "sad shires", "eyes shall shine", "tenderness of silent minds", and "glimmers of goodbyes" create a very quiet, respectful effect, as if you are speaking in church. It is as if the second half of the poem should be spoken in a quieter voice in order to show respect for the dead.

Think about this

Why wasn't Wilfred Owen famous in his own lifetime?

Today, Wilfred Owen is widely regarded as one of the finest poets of World War I, but at the time of his death, he was virtually unknown. Only four of his poems were published in his lifetime. When he was injured in 1917, he was sent to Craiglockhart War Hospital in Edinburgh. There he met one of his literary heroes, the poet and writer Siegfried Sassoon (1886–1967), who was also injured. Sassoon helped Owen with his poetry. After Owen's death, Sassoon helped to bring his work to a wider audience. If Owen had not met Sassoon in hospital, his poems would probably have been much less well known.

Some of the greatest loss of life in World War I was in the poppy fields of Flanders (present-day Belgium and northern France). Since then, red poppies have become a **symbol** for lives lost in war.

"What I Will"

Suheir Hammad is a Palestinian American writer. In "What I Will" she writes about the different actions people do in the name of their beliefs. The poem is made up of lots of short sentences, each with one main action. Try writing down all the different actions. Once you have finished reading, see how many actions you have and what you notice about them.

The importance of context

Suheir Hammad is the daughter of Palestinian refugees who emigrated to the USA when she was five years old. Palestinian refugees are those who fled their homes after the Jewish state of Israel was declared in 1948, and the war that followed between Israel and neighbouring Arab states.

More than 700,000 Palestinian Arabs – who are usually Muslims – fled from the area that became Israel. Today, those refugees live in the Palestinian territories that border Israel (the West Bank and Gaza) as well as in neighbouring Arab states and around the world. The Jewish population of Arab states also fled to Israel. The Middle East remains a region deeply troubled by conflict over land and religion. Violence frequently erupts on both sides.

Israel has built "separation barriers" along parts of its border with the Palestinian territories. Many Israelis see these barriers as vital to protect them from terrorists entering Israel. The barriers have met with widespread protest from Palestinians.

"What I Will"

by Suheir Hammad

I will not
dance to your war
drum. I will
not lend my soul nor
my bones to your war
drum. I will
not dance to your
beating. I know that beat.
It is lifeless. I know
intimately that skin
you are hitting. It
was alive once
hunted stolen
stretched. I will
not dance to your drummed
up war. I will not pop
spin beak for you. I
will not hate for you or
even hate you. I will
not kill for you. Especially
I will not die
for you. I will not mourn
the dead with murder nor
suicide. I will not side
with you nor dance to bombs
because everyone else is
dancing. Everyone can be
wrong. Life is a right not
collateral or casual. I
will not forget where
I come from. I
will craft my own drum. Gather my beloved
near and our chanting
will be dancing. Our
humming will be drumming. I
will not be played. I
will not lend my name
nor my rhythm to your
beat. I will dance
and resist and dance and
persist and dance. This heartbeat is louder than
death. Your war drum ain't
louder than this breath.

Think about this
Who is "I" and who are "you"?

"What I Will" is a poem with just one speaker addressing the reader. We hear this speaker's opinions, beliefs, and point of view. This means the poem is a **monologue**. "Mono" means one and "logue" means speech. It could be that Suheir Hammad is speaking as herself, or she could be using a made-up voice. If the speaker of the poem is "I", as in "I will not dance", who might "you" be? Who is the speaker talking to? Does the speaker agree or disagree with "your" opinions and actions?

Explaining actions

How would you explain or describe your actions to someone else? Would you be direct or would you try to explain by comparing your actions to something else? Explaining actions is tricky and, depending on what effect you want to create, you will need to use different words and images. One of the ways Suheir Hammad explains actions in "What I Will" is by using the image of a drum. The drum is an ancient symbol of war. It is also a musical instrument that gives a beat to dance to. The poet contrasts the negative war drum and the positive dance beat. This suggests that she wants the drum to be used for dancing, not for making war.

Now have a look at how the image of the drum is developed through the course of the poem. The drum image includes the drum skin, the beat it makes, the dancing it can lead, and the playing of it. As the poem nears its conclusion, the beating changes into a "heartbeat". Why do you think the poet has merged the actions of a drumbeat and a heartbeat?

The language of emotions

Can you find any words in the poem that carry strong emotions with them? How many did you find? Look at the spider diagram below and think about how you as the reader respond to this emotive language. Do you find some of the words more emotional than others?

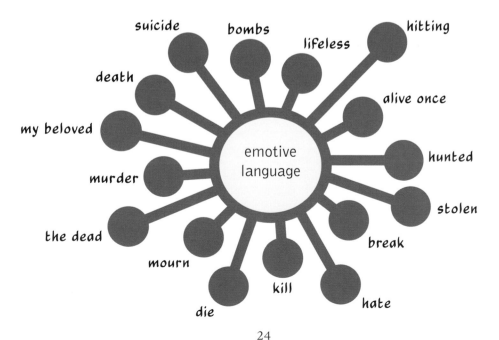

SUHEIR HAMMAD

1973–

Born: Amman, Jordan

Suheir Hammad is a poet, political **activist**, and author. She has performed her work all over the world and uses her words to change perceptions and to ask for greater understanding between people of different faiths.

Did you know? Suheir Hammad grew up in Brooklyn, New York, where she was heavily influenced by the local hip-hop scene.

Suheir Hammad writes not only about being a Palestinian and an immigrant but about being a woman struggling against sexism.

Think about this

Why repeat words and phrases?

Count how many times the speaker in "What I Will" says "I will not". Why do you think the poet has repeated this phrase so many times? Are there any other words that are also repeated a lot? Why might that be? Think about why Suheir Hammad might use very blunt, direct words: what message is she trying to get across?

Comparing poems

Comparing poems can help us to see connections between them, and make the ideas in each stand out. When you compare poems, it is helpful to choose two or three texts that have something in common, like a shared theme. For example, you could compare and contrast the theme of war as presented in "Anthem for Doomed Youth" by Wilfred Owen (on page 17) with "What I Will" by Suheir Hammad. One of the ways you might compare the poems is to look at the poetic techniques they use or their point of view. It is also useful to think about who wrote the poems and where they are from (the poems' contexts).

You will need to use a wide selection of "comparison" words when you compare poems. Meet the MAD COW and the FAT HEN! This is a really good way of remembering lots of different comparison words as well as some words that will help express your developing ideas.

M = meanwhile
A = additionally
D = during
C = consequently
O = otherwise
W = whereas

F = furthermore
A = although
T = therefore
H = however
E = even though
N = nevertheless

POINT, EVIDENCE, EXPLAIN (P.E.E.)

P.E.E. paragraphs are a useful way of writing down your ideas about poems. They have three parts:

1 This first sentence is the "point". This introduces what your paragraph is about. For example: *In "What I Will", Suheir Hammad uses lots of emotive words.*

2 Now look carefully at your poem and see what "evidence" there is to support your point. For example: *Words like "hunted", "hate", and "murder" all create a powerful response in the reader.*

3 Finally, you need to "explain" the effects of the words in the **quotation**(s). This is also where you can add in your own opinion. For example: *"Murder" and "hate" both suggest that human life is not valued. I think the poet has used these words to show how divided the Middle East is and how people are hurting each other.*

Today, it is no longer considered cowardly to oppose war. These protesters marched in opposition to the Iraq War in Washington, USA, in September 2007.

Think about this

Have attitudes to war changed?

In the past, anyone who was anti-war was considered a coward and unpatriotic. During World War I, men who refused to enlist in the army were shunned. Wilfred Owen and Siegfried Sassoon were criticized for being **pacifists** and writing about the realities of war. Many military leaders and politicians felt that their words would have a **demoralizing** effect on soldiers and the general population. A century later, however, poets like Suheir Hammad can campaign for peace without being charged with cowardice. Why do you think this change has taken place?

"The Engine"

During the late 18th and 19th centuries, developments in technology, such as steam power and new machines, transformed industry, transport, and daily life itself. Many people moved from the countryside to find work in the cities in great new factories. The Industrial Revolution is the name we give to this time, when old methods of work and family life were replaced by new ones. In "The Engine", the American poet Ella Wheeler Wilcox is writing about a steam train. However, she could equally be describing any of the new machines and their effect on human life.

Mechanical movements

Read "The Engine" to yourself. What do you notice about the way the poet describes the machine in the poem? How does it act? What movements does it make? If you look carefully, you'll see that the poet uses lots of action verbs like "darts", "speeds", and "shrieks". What do those words make you think of? What connotations do they have? Remember, the engine is a machine, so think about how we expect machines to act. Wheeler Wilcox creates a very dramatic image of the engine for her audience. Do you think she's fascinated or frightened by it? How do you feel about the engine: are you scared of this "creature"?

ELLA WHEELER WILCOX

1850–1919

Born: Johnstown, Wisconsin, USA

Wheeler Wilcox and her husband built a large home on Long Island Sound in the state of New York. They were highly sociable people and often held parties for their friends. The couple were very interested in **spiritualism**.

Did you know? Wheeler Wilcox created these famous lines in her 1883 poem "Solitude": "Laugh, and the world laughs with you; Weep, and you weep alone."

Wheeler Wilcox believed in the power of positive thinking to overcome physical illness.

"The Engine"

by Ella Wheeler Wilcox

Into the gloom of the deep, dark night,
With panting breath and a startled scream;
Swift as a bird in sudden flight
Darts this creature of steel and steam.
Awful dangers are lurking nigh,
Rocks and chasms are near the track,
But straight by the light of its great white eye
It speeds through the shadows, dense and black.
Terrible thoughts and fierce desires
Trouble its mad heart many an hour,
Where burn and smoulder the hidden fires,
Coupled ever with might and power.
It hates, as a wild horse hates the rein,
The narrow track by vale and hill;
And shrieks with a cry of startled pain,
And longs to follow its own wild will.

The machine comes to life

The engine in the poem seems to act like a human being, because it has its own "will". This means it wants to act on its own and make its own decisions, just like people do. It wants to break free from being controlled. Does the engine seem to have other feelings or even seem to be alive? When a writer makes an object appear human and gives it emotions, this is called **personification**.

Wheeler Wilcox also uses words such as "breath" and "scream" to suggest a human-like quality to the engine. The poet refers to the engine's "great white eye" and its "mad heart". In addition, the engine has "thoughts" and "desires" like a human being. What thoughts and desires might the engine have?

The opening line of the poem takes the reader into the shadowy world of the engine. The words "gloom" and "deep dark night" suggest a place where we need to be wary or watch our step. What other words make you think that you need to be careful of the engine? Could it be that the reader is also "startled" when the engine screams at the end of the poem? Do you think the poet is worried about man's ability to control the machine? Perhaps the poet is worried that machines are developing quicker than people can safely understand or control them.

Think about this
How do you feel about new technology?

Ella Wheeler Wilcox presents the engine as a monstrous force, a power that cannot be resisted. Do you think she was right to be wary of, or even fear, machines? Do you think technological development is happening too fast? Think about all the gadgets you have and how much you rely on modern technology. Do you think our lives have become technology-dependent?

Structure and speed

How is the poem structured? Look at the rhymes and punctuation, and decide how many sections there are. What about the rhythm and speed of the lines? Why do you think the poet has written them like this? Could it be to represent the clockwork actions of the engine? What happens towards the end of the poem in terms of how quickly you have to read the lines? What does this suggest about the speed and power of the engine?

THE AGE OF INDUSTRY

The Industrial Revolution started in the United Kingdom at the end of the 18th century and then spread to other countries, such as the USA, Germany, and France. Over the next 100 years, railways, bridges, and canals were built, and thousands of factories employed millions of workers. Many factories never closed: the machines kept working, and the people, including young children, worked long hours. Workers often suffered unhealthy and dangerous conditions. The great machines whirred and the floors shuddered. Many workers damaged their ears by being near noisy machinery. Note all the sound words used in "The Engine" to create the noise of the machine.

Supervised by an overseer, a child worker operates a giant spinning machine.

"Acts of God"

When you read the title of this poem, what do you think an "act of God" might be? Does it strike you as a good thing or a bad thing? This poem has two parts to it. The two parts are connected by a shared theme. As you read the two parts, think about what the poet, Heather McHugh, is calling an act of God. Was it what you expected it to be?

Exploring titles and theme

Heather McHugh has called the two parts of her poem "Tornado" and "Lightning". What ideas do these words suggest to you? Both words refer to unpredictable and powerful weather that can wreak havoc and destroy lives. However, do you think of them as having the same power or is one more powerful than the other? Think about a tornado being a massive build-up of pressure before it spins out of control, while a lightning strike is quick and dramatic.

The title "Acts of God" refers to events like tornadoes and lightning that are beyond human control. These are often beyond our power to even predict. We label actions like these "acts of God" as a way of explaining their randomness.

"Acts of God"
by Heather McHugh

I. Tornado
I said the people come inside.
They would be safe in the room.
So many of those people die.
You can see my guilt.

I could see
hands to a lady moving.
I knew the lady.
You can see my guilt.

Sometimes I want to run, to get
away from it. I ask forgiveness
night and day. I ask it from
the cemetery. I can never
dream this storm away.

It was over for maybe minutes.
Then it was never over.

II. Lightning
It pushed me backward, I could see
my friends go backward too,
as from a blast, but slowly,
very slowly, everything
was in a different time.

It burned inside my body.
I could feel my hands
curl up. My pocket got
on fire. I didn't want to reach in there
and take a handful of the hot: my money hurt.

I'm different now forever. Put that fact
into your book. My hair used to be straight.
My eyes – you see? They're gray as ash.
They used to be light blue. You live,

if you're lucky, but take my word:
It changes how you look.

HEATHER McHUGH
1948–
Born: San Diego, California, USA

Heather McHugh has written poetry
since the age of five. She is one of the
USA's most respected poets and has
received many prizes and awards for
her work.

Did you know? McHugh's first poem
had been published in the famous
New Yorker magazine by the time she
was 20.

McHugh considers that being an expert "eavesdropper" is essential to her poetry.

The poetic voice

Who or what do you think could be the narrator of "Tornado" and "Lightning"? Do both parts of the poem have the same narrator or **poetic voice**? The phrase "You can see my guilt" is repeated twice in "Tornado", which **implies** that the narrator is a person who is to blame for the tornado. If so, who could that be? Who is "you" referring to? Is it a human or do you think it could be a force like the wind itself? Could the poet be personifying the wind?

Look further into the way the parts are written. "Tornado" is written by a person or voice who is doing all the actions and making them happen. In contrast, the narrator of "Lightning" is **passive** and having the actions done to her, as in "It pushed me backward". Could the theme of the second section, then, be suffering? What do you think?

Actions and consequences

When you think of a tornado, you probably imagine a mighty whirlwind tearing up everything in its path. But in "Tornado", the storm is never described and the actions are **inferred** rather than shown. We see the consequences of the tornado's actions in terms of the "cemetery" and people dying. However, we never see the storm itself, which might be a clue to the poem's meaning.

All actions have consequences. In the two parts of "Acts of God", the poet shows the different after-effects of the tornado and lightning. The tornado causes deaths, while the lightning "changes" people. What do you think the "changes" might be?

ASKING QUESTIONS

With more abstract and challenging poems, it is useful to ask lots of questions of a poem in order to begin to make sense of it. Ask yourself the following questions and see if you come up with any conclusions. Don't worry if you don't reach a definite conclusion. Exploring possibilities is what makes poetry fascinating.

- In "Tornado", could the voice be that of the tornado itself?
- Is the narrator a person who somehow takes responsibility for the storm?
- If so, why would a human take the blame for an act of God?
- Why might they feel guilty?
- Is the tornado real or a metaphor?
- If the tornado is a metaphor, what could the tornado represent?
- Is the poetic voice in "Lightning" human?
- Could the lightning be a metaphor, too?

Emotive language

Can you find any emotive language in "Acts of God"? What about "die", "guilt", and "forgiveness" in "Tornado"? These words nearly always provoke a response in us because we associate negative emotions with them. Can you find any emotive words in "Lightning"? Words like "burned" and "hurt" suggest physical pain, but do you think the poetic voice is emotional about these words? Or is the narrator more matter of fact about them?

Playing around with punctuation

Some modern poetry is written in **free verse**, which means that it is not written in neat sections with a regular pattern of punctuation, rhyme, and rhythm. "Acts of God" is written in stanzas, but examine what happens to the punctuation after the first stanza. Look at stanza 3 again:

Sometimes I want to run, to get
away from it. I ask forgiveness
night and day. I ask it from
the cemetery. I can never
dream this storm away.

Look at how the first words of lines 2, 3, 4, and 5 are emphasized by having to read on to finish the sentence at the full stop. Can you spot where the rhymes are? Does that change how you read it out loud? Why do you think the poet chose to begin a new line when she did?

Time references

In both sections of "Acts of God", there are references to time. In "Tornado", there is "night and day" and "never over", both implying a continual storm or action. In "Lightning", the time references are more subtle. We are told that the action happened "slowly, very slowly" and that it was in a "different time". These suggest a blurred memory. We are also given the past and the present. So, we learn about the lightning strike and what it is like "now".

Think about this

Can this poem be compared to any others?

How does this poem compare to any of the others you have read so far in this book? Does it have similar powerful emotions to Wilfred Owen's "Anthem for Doomed Youth" (on page 17)? Or does it compare better with the voice of "What I Will" (on page 23), with its forceful **first person** narrator? Perhaps "Acts of God" reminds you of another poem you know. What makes it similar? Does it share a theme or a style?

In May 2011, a tornado hit Joplin in the US state of Missouri, killing 158 and severely damaging the city's hospital.

"Caged Bird"

Maya Angelou wrote her poem "Caged Bird" in the early 1980s. At that time, many African Americans still felt that their rights were ignored by the US government, despite the great advances made by the **civil rights** movement of the 1960s. High-profile cases of police **brutality** against African Americans hit the headlines, and several American cities experienced race riots. As you read this poem, think about the different actions of the two birds, the free bird and the caged bird.

Interpreting metaphors

Look carefully at the words that the poet uses to describe the actions of the two birds. What or who do you think the two birds might represent? Angelou does not mention race anywhere in the poem, but many people interpret the poem's birds metaphor as representing black and white people. This suggests that the poem's themes are race and inequality. What might the "wind" refer to? Some people think it is a metaphor for history and the general case that, in the past, white people in the USA have had more opportunities than black people. Think about the actions performed on the caged bird, such as its "clipped wings". Who has done that, and why? What action can the caged bird take now?

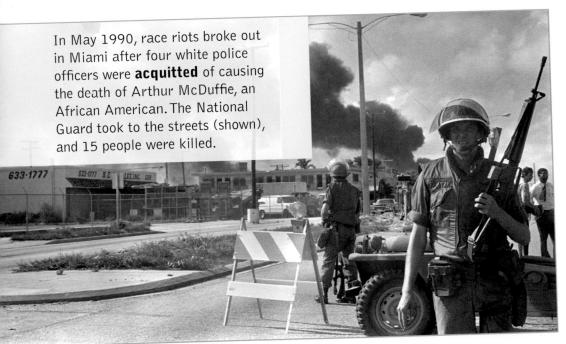

In May 1990, race riots broke out in Miami after four white police officers were **acquitted** of causing the death of Arthur McDuffie, an African American. The National Guard took to the streets (shown), and 15 people were killed.

"Caged Bird"

by Maya Angelou

A free bird leaps
on the back of the wind
and floats downstream
till the current ends
and dips his wing
in the orange sun rays
and dares to claim the sky.

But a bird that stalks
down his narrow cage
can seldom see through
his bars of rage
his wings are clipped and
his feet are tied
so he opens his throat to sing.

The caged bird sings
with a fearful trill
of things unknown
but longed for still
and his tune is heard
on the distant hill
for the caged bird
sings of freedom.

The free bird thinks of another breeze
and the trade winds soft through the sighing trees
and the fat worms waiting on a dawn bright lawn
and he names the sky his own
But a caged bird stands on the grave of dreams
his shadow shouts on a nightmare scream
his wings are clipped and his feet are tied
so he opens his throat to sing.

The caged bird sings
with a fearful trill
of things unknown
but longed for still
and his tune is heard
on the distant hill
for the caged bird
sings of freedom.

MAYA ANGELOU

1928–

Born: St Louis, Missouri, USA

Maya Angelou is a poet, writer, teacher, dancer, dramatist, and civil rights campaigner. In the 1960s, she campaigned alongside African American civil rights leaders Malcolm X and Martin Luther King for equality between white Americans and African Americans.

Did you know? Maya Angelou's autobiography, *I Know Why the Caged Bird Sings*, is studied in schools all over the world. In it, she describes her childhood and her struggles to overcome abuse, single parenthood, and racism.

In 2011, Maya Angelou was awarded the Presidential Medal of Freedom by President Barack Obama. It is the USA's highest honour for **civilians.**

The language of action and emotion

The two main actions described in Angelou's poem are flying and singing. The free bird is highly active and can roam the skies, leaping and dipping, while the caged bird can only sing. The free bird "dares to claim the sky", which suggests power and freedom. This is in direct contrast to the other bird, which sits in its "narrow cage" with its "clipped" wings and "tied" feet.

Perhaps singing is a metaphor for taking control of one's own destiny. Even though the caged bird cannot open its cage and can only sing with a "fearful trill", it still "opens" its throat and "sings of freedom". The caged bird is forced to see through "his bars of rage". Notice how the poet hints at a simmering anger that threatens to overspill as the bird "stalks" in his cage.

Singing for freedom

In this poem, perhaps Maya Angelou is encouraging African Americans to build on the progress already made with civil rights and to continue the struggle towards equality. The lack of punctuation and the rapid rhythm reflect a sense of urgency to make this happen. The poet wants the reader to remember the struggles of African Americans in the past. She writes of the "grave of dreams", to represent all the people who died hoping for equality and never getting it. Perhaps Angelou is encouraging black people to sing loudly (or protest and act) so that their "tune is heard on the distant hill". The "hill" could refer to Capitol Hill, which is the area where the US government sits and makes laws.

SLAVERY AND SEGREGATION

Racial **segregation** in the United States goes back to the days when America was a British colony and the first African slaves were imported and forced to work for white people. Slavery was officially abolished throughout the USA in 1865. However, strict segregation still existed in many states. Local laws were passed that declared that black and white people still had to live apart and use separate public facilities, such as parks, schools, shops, and buses. White people usually had more opportunities and more freedom, and as a result were wealthier. In the 1950s and 60s, people like Martin Luther King led a civil rights movement demanding change. In 1964, the Civil Rights Act marked an end to major forms of legal discrimination including segregation.

An African American drinks from a "colored" drinking fountain in Oklahoma, USA, in 1939.

Action and power

Look again at "Caged Bird" and you will see that the free bird can act as it pleases. It "leaps" and "floats" and "dips" because it chooses to. Now read once more the stanzas describing the caged bird. Does it act according to its own choices or does it have actions done to it? Who has put the bird in the cage? Who has clipped its wings and tied its feet? Notice all the words in the poem connected with the theme of imprisonment.

However, the caged bird's "tune is heard". Do you think the poet is optimistic about the future? Do you think Angelou believes that action can change things? The caged bird sings for "things unknown but longed for still". What might the "things unknown" be? Perhaps the bird is singing for the chance to do all the things the free bird does and be equal.

FOCUS ON ONE STANZA

A useful technique is to home in closely on one particular stanza of a poem, to see what light it sheds on the poem as a whole. In the fourth stanza of "Caged Bird", key contrasts are made between the two birds. The free bird "names the sky his own", which suggests he has claimed his place confidently in the world. Perhaps this also suggests white people excluding black people and dominating them. The free bird can also claim "fat worms", suggesting all the opportunities open to white people. Meanwhile, the caged bird "shouts on a nightmare scream" and "stands on the grave of dreams". The "grave of dreams" is an emotive metaphor for lost hope, while the "nightmare scream" suggests the long-held frustration at being "caged".

Martin Luther King (1929–68) was a key leader of the US civil rights movement. He urged African Americans to protest using non-violent means. In 1999, his history-making 1963 "I have a dream" speech was honoured on a US stamp.

Think about this

What if you were the caged bird?

Imagine if you couldn't sit where you wanted on a bus, or were told you had to go to a separate school from your friends. What if you couldn't play in the same park, go to the same swimming pool, or sit in the same café as other people? If you were the caged bird, what action would you take? Now think about "Caged Bird" in relation to "What I Will" (on page 23). How are the two poets trying to bring about changes? How do they use their voices differently? Which actions do you think are more powerful?

"Not My Business"

If something is "not your business", it's a way of saying it has nothing to do with you. Think about how this might be relevant to the poem as you read it. What actions are being witnessed? Think about what Niyi Osundare is saying about the consequences of not acting. What might he be telling us about human nature along the way?

The poem's context

Many poets use their poetic voice to write about politically motivated actions. In "Not My Business", Niyi Osundare informs the reader of the danger of ignoring a political threat until it is too late. The political theme of the poem reflects its context. Osundare wrote the poem as a criticism of the **dictatorship** in Nigeria. From 1993 to 1998, General Sani Abacha led a brutal **regime** in the country. During this period, poetry was considered a very dangerous activity and many writers were imprisoned or even tortured.

Think about this
Who are "They"?

The poem begins with the simple word "They", but who do you think "They" are? Could "They" be soldiers? Police officers? We never find out their identity but we do find out how dangerous "They" are. We know that "They" are violent because of the **dynamic** verbs the poet uses to describe their actions: "beat", "stuffed", "booted", "dragged". These words are physical movements and all have negative connotations. If you say these four words out loud, what effect do they have?

"Not My Business"

by Niyi Osundare

They picked Akanni up one morning
Beat him soft like clay
And stuffed him down the belly
Of a waiting jeep.

What business of mine is it
So long they don't take the yam
From my savouring mouth?

They came one night
Booted the whole house awake
And dragged Danladi out,
Then off to a lengthy absence.

What business of mine is it
So long they don't take the yam
From my savouring mouth?

Chinwe went to work one day
Only to find her job was gone:
No query, no warning, no probe –
Just one neat sack for a stainless record.

What business of mine is it
So long they don't take the yam
From my savouring mouth?

And then one evening
As I sat down to eat my yam
A knock on the door froze my hungry hand.

The jeep was waiting on my bewildered lawn
Waiting, waiting in its usual silence.

No escape

How many references to time can you see in the poem? When do the events and actions take place? We read that the first event happened in the morning. This is followed by one at night, another in the day, and the last one in the evening. If "They" can come at any time, is anyone safe?

In the poem, Osundare shows that no one can escape the political situation. Akanni, Danladi, and Chinwe are all ordinary people who, like the poem's narrator, get caught up in circumstances that they have no control over. The threat of being taken or being affected by the authorities for no reason is best shown in the verse about Chinwe. She is sacked from her job despite there being no complaints: "no query, no warning, no probe". Her "stainless record" is not enough to protect her from the brutal regime.

The effect of making objects human

Look back at the way Osundare describes the jeep in the poem. What do you notice? Are there any surprises there? You will see that the jeep "They" drive has a "belly". Which part of the jeep do you think the "belly" refers to? Why do you think the writer chose this word rather than another? Through using the word "belly", the poet is making the jeep like a human – he is personifying it. The "belly" gobbles up Akanni and will, at the end of the poem, do the same for the narrator.

Compare how Osundare personifies the jeep in this poem with how Ella Wheeler Wilcox makes the steam train human in "The Engine" (on page 29). Both machines are presented as threats to people. It is as if the two machines are out of control and threaten to take action on their own.

Should all writers be free to write what they like?

There are people all over the world who live under strict or **repressive** regimes. If the government in these countries thinks someone is a threat, they may arrest them, just as in Osundare's poem. Writers in these countries sometimes have their books **censored** or even banned if the authorities consider them dangerous. Ken Saro-Wiwa was a famous Nigerian writer and campaigner who was hanged in 1995 for speaking out against the authorities. Should writers be free to write whatever they like?

NIYI OSUNDARE

1947–

Born: Ikere-Ekiti, Nigeria

Niyi Osundare is a poet and playwright. He sees words as actions and writes about many important issues such as racial equality and **free speech**.

Did you know? When he was teaching at Ibadan University in Nigeria, some of Osundare's students were informers for the military regime that ruled the country. The authorities were suspicious of Osundare because he wrote poetry that sometimes criticized them.

Osundare once said that "to utter is to alter", and much of his poetry is concerned with using the power of words to make a difference.

The power of words and actions

Think about words and how powerful they can be sometimes, from hurtful words to loving ones. Now think about actions and how we sometimes judge and are judged by them. For example, doing a kind act will not just make you feel good but it may have a direct impact on someone else and what they think of you. What about unkind acts or even failing to act? How can that change people's opinions of you?

Exploring hints

Investigating possible meanings by looking at the word clues and hints is a fun way to explore poems. Look back at the end of the poem's third stanza. Danladi is dragged out of his house and taken "off to a lengthy absence". What do you think a "lengthy absence" could mean? Could it mean prison or something even worse? Why doesn't the poet tell us directly what he means?

The poet chooses to soften the harsh reality by being vague and unclear. People do this all the time in daily life, particularly when they are talking about sensitive issues like death or illness. For example, we might say "passed away" or "at peace" to avoid sounding shocking or having to think too hard about the truth of death. We do not know for sure what has happened to Danladi, but from the rest of the poem, we can guess that it is not good. The vague speech also suggests that the narrator is afraid to speak too clearly – and to speak up about what is really happening. Doing so would attract the attention of the authorities.

Are there any places where the poet does use very direct, harsh language? What about "stuffed" and "booted"? The violent and aggressive words to describe actions in the poem are like those used by Wilfred Owen in "Anthem for Doomed Youth" (on page 17). Are both Owen and Osundare using these harsh words to comment on the same kinds of actions? How do the poets want their readers to respond? Try to use some MAD COW FAT HEN (see page 26) words to express your ideas.

Think about this
Whose business is it?

If it is not the narrator's business to act and be concerned about what is happening to other people, whose business is it? Look closely at the poem's chorus. How is the repeated line "What business of mine is it" used by Osundare to create a sense of judgement in the reader? As we read, we have a strong feeling of outrage at what "They" are doing. However, we are also shocked by the narrator's lack of action. His refusal to act can make him appear almost as bad as the thugs who are taking people away. Do you think the narrator is really selfish or is he just protecting himself? Think about human nature and how we have a strong instinct to look after ourselves. Should we judge the narrator or should we think about what we might do in the same situation?

These women protesters are holding posters with photos of their loved-ones who "disappeared" (like Akanni and Danladi) during the regime of General Pinochet in Chile (1973–1990). Their posters read "Donde Estan?", which means "Where are they?"

What have we learned?

Action poems cover many different ideas, movements, forms, and styles. Remember that poetic techniques, themes, and structure are just part of the toolkit at a poet's disposal. Depending on the purpose, audience, and context, the poet will decide which "tools" to use. When you are reading a poem, begin with whatever facts or details you know and work from there. It is also good to be open-minded about a poem and to not panic about not understanding it.

Keep an open mind

The best approach to a poem is to explore different possibilities or **interpretations**. Think about how many ways the actions in the poem can be seen, done, interpreted, and misinterpreted. At first, remember to concentrate on the lines and images you do understand – just work with those. Later, when you've looked at the poem a few more times, other ideas and meanings will start to emerge. It's very rare to understand a poem on the first reading. Poets want you to read their work a few times. Reading a poem is a different process from reading a novel.

Find the light

Using the tools and approaches you have already discovered in this book, you will have the confidence to explore a new poem, even if you do not know exactly what everything **signifies** or means. Sometimes you won't understand every word and you will need to look some up in a dictionary. Always think about what the words mean to you. What images do the words conjure up in your mind? How do those words and images make you think or feel?

If you do all of this, you won't stay in the darkness for long. Try using the question chart opposite to help you approach a new poem – and shed light on the poet's purpose.

Think about this
Have your opinions changed?

Look back at the poems in this book and think about the thoughts and feelings you had about them when you read them for the first time. Then think about all that you've read, learned, and considered about them since that first reading. Has your opinion changed about any of the poems? Or are you still thinking and reflecting and making up your mind? Whatever stage you are at, enjoy your exploring!

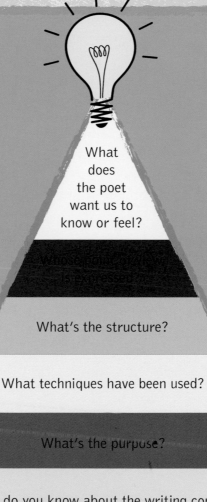

What does the poet want us to know or feel?

Whose point of view is expressed?

What's the structure?

What techniques have been used?

What's the purpose?

What do you know about the writing context?

Look at the title early on. Consider the theme.

What else is there to explore?

Which was your favourite poem in this book? What was so special about it? Did you like its clever use of techniques or did you admire the way the attitudes and opinions were expressed? There's an action poem for every single mood, attitude, and moment. If you liked the poems in this book and want to explore more, then try some of the following suggestions:

- If you liked "Paul Revere's Ride", then you might like another galloping, dramatic narrative poem called "The Charge of the Light Brigade", by Alfred, Lord Tennyson (1809–1892). You will hear galloping horses again, but you will also hear cannon fire, witness battlefield slaughter, and get a real sense of pity and wasted lives.
- If you want to read more of Wilfred Owen's poetry, read his famous "Dulce et Decorum Est". Don't be put off by the Latin title: the poem narrates a poisonous gas attack in the trenches in World War I. Owen is using the Latin motto (*Dulce et decorum est pro patria mori*, meaning "It is sweet and noble to die for one's country") in a bitterly ironic way.
- What about Maya Angelou's "Caged Bird"? If you liked that poem, you could find some other poems that explore African American history and civil rights. Try "Praise Song for the Day" by Elizabeth Alexander (1962–), which was written to mark the occasion of Barack Obama's presidential **inauguration** in 2009.

In his 1854 poem "The Charge of the Light Brigade", Tennyson wrote about a doomed British **cavalry** charge against Russian cannon during the Crimean War (1853–56).

- If you liked the metaphor and mystery of "Acts of God", then read more of Heather McHugh's poetry, such as in her 2009 collection *Upgraded to Serious*. Her themes include love, loss, and those small **domestic** actions that change people.
- If "What I Will" by Suheir Hammad and "Not My Business" by Niyi Osundare struck a chord with you, then try "Revenge" by Nicaraguan poet Luis Enrique Mejía Godoy (1945–). This is another poem about political actions. However, in this poem, someone who was imprisoned and tortured later meets their captor on the street. How would you expect them to react? Read the poem and find out if you guessed right.
- If you enjoyed "The Engine" by Ella Wheeler Wilcox, you could read the sinister "The Secret of the Machines" by Rudyard Kipling (1865–1936), in which machines start to take over the world.

Have any of these poems inspired you to take action? To protest about something you care about, like protecting our environment? To explore something new? To write your own poem?

Think about this
Is an action's meaning always clear?

Remember that actions can have many different interpretations. Imagine someone shaking a clenched fist. What could that mean? Could it be a fight about to happen? A gesture of commitment to a cause? A response to bad news? Or could it be pain?

Write your own action poem

Writing poetry is fun. Playing with style and words until you get down on paper exactly what you want to say is an exciting challenge. Remember that actions can be small or large, domestic or global, witnessed or reported. Think about all the poems in the book and look back to see what ideas, actions, and techniques your favourite ones used.

Here are 10 easy steps that can help you write your own amazing action poem:

1. Find a quiet space free from distractions. Gather together paper and pens and set up your writer's desk. (Tip: It's good to sit near a window where you can look out and get inspiration.)

2. Choose one aspect of action from the spider diagram on page 4. Think carefully about your choice. The more you can identify with your chosen theme the better. For example, you might be a soldier fighting in a war or someone making a protest against something.

3. How are you going to represent that action? For example, if you are going to write about machines, are you going to use a metaphor? (Tip: Note down all your ideas. Don't cross anything out at this stage. The more ideas you have to choose from, the better.)

4. Now think about the structure you want to use. Do you want to go for free verse or are you going to set yourself the challenge of sticking to the sonnet form like Wilfred Owen? (Tip: If you are going to write a sonnet, it's a good idea to map out the lines and rhyme scheme before you begin.)

5. What techniques will be most effective and relevant to use? If you're going to write about a mechanical object then **onomatopoeia**, personification, **similes**, and metaphors might best create the sound and description. If you're writing about something more personal, like protest, then you might want to use emotive language and other techniques used by Maya Angelou and Suheir Hammad.

6. What's your title going to be? Is it going to be straightforward, like "The Engine", or mysterious like "Acts of God"?

7. What's your writing purpose? Is it to protest or inform, entertain or suggest?

8. Who is your audience? Is it younger children, adults, or people your own age?

9. Look back at all the notes you've got so far. Which ones do you want to keep? Which ones are you going to save for another poem?

10. Take a deep breath. Feel how your body moves as you breathe. Think about your five senses and how they react. OK? Now you're ready to start writing!

Crafting your writing

Once you've got a first draft of your poem, you're ready to start shaping, or crafting, your writing. Almost nobody writes exactly what they want to first time around, so most poets craft their work. They check their word and technique choices to ensure they make maximum impact on their audience.

Read through the following hints and tips for perfecting your poem. If you use a different coloured pen to craft your poem from the one you used to write it, you will see the changes happening really clearly:

- Is your title too easy or too difficult? Is there a better title for what you've written? Experiment with different titles and see which one best creates the effect you want.
- Have you used any "extra words" that aren't doing anything? Extra words are words like "really", "nice", and "very". Do you have any of these? Can you delete them? Don't delete too many – your audience still has to understand!
- Does your poem sound the way you want it to? Read it aloud to yourself first and then to a friend. Ask your audience for their feedback. Would it be a good idea to add more sound effects?
- How does your poem look on the page? Are you happy with its structure? What happens if you change it from, for example, free verse into a sonnet? Is the meaning lost or improved?
- Use a thesaurus to help you choose even more precise describing words. This will help you to pinpoint your details.
- If you haven't included a metaphor or a simile, can you add one in? What does that add to the effect of your poem?
- Ask a friend to listen to your poem. What does he/she think the theme is? What suggestions does he/she have for improving your poem?
- It's a good idea to leave your poem for a while and go and do something else. Reflection time is a really important part of writing a poem. Go for a walk and come back to the poem later or even in a few days' time. You'll be fresh and more perceptive about your work.
- Do you think your reader will feel the emotions you want? Can you shape your word choices to make them more extreme or more emotive?
- If you aren't happy with your poem, you can always try again. It's not supposed to be a quick fix!

What is your
inspiration for
your action poem?

GREEN FOR HOPE

The Chilean **Nobel Prize**-winning poet
Pablo Neruda (1904–1973) always wrote
in green ink because he thought that
green was the colour of hope. Maybe
green ink will inspire you too!

Bibliography

The following works provided important sources of information for this book:

Hinge and Sign, Heather McHugh (Wesleyan University Press, 1994)

I Remember, I Remember: Favourite Poems from Childhood, editors Rob Farrow and Jennifer Curry (Red Fox, 1993)

The Little Book of War Poems, editor Nick de Somogyi (Siena, 1999)

More Poetry Please (Phoenix, 1993)

The New Oxford Book of Verse, editor Helen Gardner (Oxford University Press, 1989)

The Oxford Companion to Children's Literature, editors Humphrey Carpenter and Mari Prichard (Oxford University Press, 1995)

The Oxford Companion to English Literature, editor Margaret Drabble (Oxford University Press, 2006)

The Oxford Companion to English Poetry, editor Ian Hamilton (Oxford University Press, 1994)

The Poems of Wilfred Owen (Wordsworth Editions, 1994)

The Prentice Hall Guide to English Literature, editor Marion Wynne-Davies (Prentice Hall, 1990)

Shaker, Why Don't You Sing?, Maya Angelou (Random House, 1983)

ZaatarDiva, Suheir Hammad (Cypher Books, 2005)

Glossary

abstract theoretical, not concrete or proved

acquitted declared not guilty

activist someone who takes direct action on an issue, by going on a protest march or campaigning for political or environmental change

alliteration when two or more words near each other begin with the same sound

brutality cruelty or violence

cavalry soldiers on horseback

censored removed, deleted, or banned because it is considered a threat to security or morality

civilian person not in the armed forces or police force

civil rights every person's right to freedom and equality in all areas

civil war war between people within the same country

colony region ruled by another country

Congress United States parliament: the House of Representatives and the Senate

connotation implied meaning of a word or phrase

context background setting, circumstances, or conditions

couplet pair of lines in a poem that usually rhyme and are the same length

demoralizing making people feel hopeless

dictatorship country ruled by a powerful person, usually by force

domestic relating to the home or family life

dynamic energetic, powerful

economical unwasteful

emotive causing emotion

epitaph words engraved on a gravestone

eulogy speech of praise given after someone has died

first person the person speaking; making use of "I" and "me"

free speech legal right to express any opinion in public

free verse poetry without a fixed structure or pattern, with lines of varying length

implies strongly hints or suggests

inauguration formal ceremony to place someone in an official position, like the President of the United States

inferred concluded from looking at the evidence

interpretation possible meaning

metaphor comparison between things that are unlike each other without using a word such as "like" or "as"

monologue speech or one-sided conversation by a poet, character, or other writer or speaker

motivated driven, or caused to act

Nobel Prize international award given in recognition of artistic, social, or scientific achievements

onomatopoeia word that sounds like what it describes

pacifist person who does not believe in war and refuses to perform military service

passive not active; unreacting

patriot someone who loves their country and is prepared to defend it vigorously

patriotic strongly supporting your own country

personification giving a non-human object human characteristics and/or emotions

poetic licence using facts in a creative way

poetic voice narrator, who is speaking or voicing the poem

Poet Laureate poet chosen by the head of state to write poetry for important occasions like a royal wedding

quotation copying of words that have already been written by someone else; they should be put in single or double quotation marks

regime strict and severe government

repressive controlling; preventing freedom

requiem religious service or music for someone who has died

segregation separation of racial, religious, or ethnic groups by enforcing separate schools, transport, housing, and other facilities

semantic field group of words all on the same topic, such as war or romance

shell shock mental health disorder caused by exposure to warfare, especially shellfire

signifies stands for, or means

simile comparison of one thing with another of a different kind, using a word such as "like" or "as"; for example, "her eyes twinkled like stars"

sonnet poem of 14 lines, often with 10 syllables per line

spiritualism belief that the spirits of the dead can communicate with the living

stanza set of lines within a poem; all the stanzas within a poem may have the same form (e.g. the same rhyme scheme) or they may vary

syllable word or part of a word that has a separate sound when you say it; for example, "protest" (pro-test) has two syllables

symbol thing that has a meaning beyond what it actually is

symbolize represent, or stand for

tempo speed

theme key idea that the poet wants the reader to think about

War of Independence war between the United States and Great Britain from 1775 to 1783

Find out more

Poetry websites

There are lots of great poetry websites. Here are some to check out:

http://mayaangelou.com
To discover more about the poet, author, and activist's life, have a look at her official website.

www.bbc.co.uk/schools
The BBC Schools' learning hub has lots of information about poetry, as well as plenty of really great poems to read and enjoy.

www.loc.gov/poetry/180
The American poet Billy Collins created the online poetry resource Poetry 180 for high schools in the USA. There is a poem for each day of the school year.

www.hwlongfellow.org
If you are lucky enough to visit Maine, USA, you could go to Henry Wadsworth Longfellow's house. You can also find out more about the poet at this website.

www.oucs.ox.ac.uk/ww1lit
At the First World War Poetry Digital Archive, you can listen to recordings, view images, and see films connected to the poets and poetry of World War I.

www.wilfredowen.org.uk
Find out more information about the life and poetry of Wilfred Owen.

What to read

You will find poetry books on many different subjects in your local library or bookshop. Don't forget to read the poems aloud.

How to Eat a Poem by Ted Kooser (Dover Publications, 2009)
This has a range of poems on all sorts of subjects, including actions, adventure, and travel.

Heroes: 100 Poems from the New Generation of War Poets edited by John Jeffcock (Ebury Press, 2011)
The poems in this collection are written by soldiers on active duty today. There are also some by children and wives of soldiers.

A Laureate's Choice: 101 Poems for Children by Carol Ann Duffy (Macmillan Children's Books, 2013)
Poet Laureate Carol Ann Duffy has selected a fantastic range of poems on a variety of topics.

The Oxford Treasury of Classic Poems (Oxford University Press, 2011)
A collection of some of the most famous poems of all time.

Where the Sidewalk Ends by Shel Silverstein (Particular Books, 2010)
The popular poet writes poems about childhood and some of the actions, concerns, and adventures children experience.

Other topics to research

Sometimes a poem is written to mark an important action or event in a country's history. This might be a royal wedding, a monarch dying, a key political decision, a new law, or a war. These poems are often written by the Poet Laureate of the day. You could research Poet Laureates from the past and present and find out what important actions they chose to write poems about.

www.englishpen.org
If you liked "Not My Business" and you are interested in Niyi Osundare's life in Nigeria, you could find out more about writers who live and work under strict governments on this site.

Picture acknowledgements
We would like to thank the following for permission to reproduce photographs:
Cover photograph: Shutterstock/djgis.
Corbis: pp. 31 and 38 (Bettmann); Dreamstime.com: pp. 8 (Americanspirit), 10 (Lukovic), 19 (Lochstampfer), 32–33 (Fotolottl), 36 (Floydine), 42 (Baggett), 53 (DMC Design); Getty Images: pp. 6 (Scott J. Ferrell), 16 (General Photographic Agency/Hulton), 18 (Fotosearch), 25 (Bryan Bedder), 40 (Chip Somodevilla); John Trumbull: p. 15; Library of Congress: p. 52; Mac Foundation: p. 33; Mary Evans: p. 28 (Everett Collection); Museum of Fine Arts, Boston: p. 14; Museum of Memory and Human Rights: p. 49; National Library of Scotland: p. 20; Niyi Osundare: p. 47; Ragesoss: p. 27; Russell Lee: p.41; Shutterstock: pp. 1 (Frenkel), 3 (Konoval), 5 (Wrangel), 9 (Mamahoohooba), 21 (Schier), 26 (Tischenko), 29 (Rambleon), 30 (Elisseeva), 34–35 (Insogna), 37 (Brandes), 39 (Zhuda), 43 (axz700), 45 (Greek Studio), 46 (Doroshin), 48 (Cross), 50 (Mango Juicy), 54 (GrafVision), 57t (Wickland), 57b (Popova); SuperStock: pp. 13 (Thomas Buchanan Read), 44 (Stocktrek Images); W. Hagens: p. 22.

Index